STUCK
IN THE
MIDDLE

WHEN BOTH OF YOUR PARENTS ARE NARCISSISTS

DAWN JEWELL

Stuck in the Middle When Both of Your Parents Are Narcissists

By

Dawn Jewell

ISBN

Paperback: 979-8-90190-221-9

Hardcover: 979-8-90190-222-6

Dedication

When you find a therapist who listens without making your insane life seem episodic, you ought to keep her and mention her in your book when you write it.

Thank you, K.S. You have been exactly what I needed.

Acknowledgments

When you read a book, you always see the acknowledgement section and wonder who reads it. I know I used to skim it, but now that I've written my own book and have so many people to thank, I hope you're taking the time to read this little section.

To my husband, thank you for all the things. For your strength, your belief in me, your ability to roll through all the parts of our life with grace and laughter, and for not laughing at me when I said I was going to write a book.

To my kids…R, D, and C. You three, your father, and I will always be the core five. Thank you for loving me even though I know I wasn't always perfect, and especially when I lost my shit. Thank you for being willing to smile at family pictures, to be honest with your thoughts and feelings, and for loving each other in a way my sister and I don't know how to do. And honestly, thank you for remembering the rules and not embarrassing mommy in public as children, and especially now as adults!

To my grands…K, M, C, J, and W, the five of you keep us on our toes, and I cannot wait to see what you all become! I also can't wait to see what you teach any grands that come after you. Always know Papa and me are just a phone call away.

To S. Y., P.H., and P.B., thank you each for being a true friend. I can reach out to you without fear of judgment and the knowledge that you'll tell me the truth, even if it hurts, and the fact that you each give me back the love I have for you. Finding your true tribe is so difficult, and you all have stood with me through so many years! Now, if we just lived closer, that would be great, please and thank you!

To the G. Family…thank you for loving my husband so much that you went ahead and loved me too after I fell into his life at your racetrack back in 1999. Thank you for the snazzy white GUESS jeans and red "Speedway Official" shirt you made him wear and for giving me that to tease him about so many times over the years. Thank you for being our chosen family and for loving us unconditionally. Pat, I hope you're reading this from above and know how much you are missed and how thankful I am for your kids and your husband, who have become my people.

To M.B., thank you for accepting me into your village, for introducing me to so many new friends, and for understanding the important role grandmas play in the world. You are a beautiful gift, and I'm so glad I got to know you and your Blooms. You are truly the Magic Maker, sweet friend…don't ever forget that!

And finally, to K.S., you were the first therapist (of five!) to listen carefully and constantly call me on my bull shit. You laugh with me, and you've seen me cry. You've asked me to look at things in a different light, and when everything looked like it had gone to shit, you brainstormed the idea for this book with me! I hope it lives up to what you thought it could be, and I hope you recommend it to a client one day! See you at GMA, friend!

About the Author

Dawn is a mom of three, grandma to five, and wife to one amazing man. When the idea for this book came up, she talked to her husband and kids and asked their opinion on sharing this story. They supported her without question. She currently lives in Northern Virginia and enjoys spending time with her family, sitting in the sun, camping in her RV, and naming all kinds of inanimate objects so everyone must remember the name of the mower, the RV, the golf cart, etc.

She's still healing from damage she really didn't know she had until late in life, and sometimes it feels like that process will never end. There will never be enough time to be thankful for all the beauty in life, and her only wish is that she can be half the grandmother to her babies that Dorothy was to her, and that her children never have to heal from her.

Table of Contents

The Pilot

As a child, you do not understand the word stuck, but as you grow, you understand the depth of this word. Stuck means being unable to move or progress due to being fixed in place. It might be because you glued something, taped it up, or cemented it in place. Or it could be that you're unable to remove yourself from a situation, thinking it would cause more trouble than it's worth. Something similar to a loveless relationship.

But in the second instance, I would argue that you're only as stuck as you want to be, and almost anything can be unstuck if you're willing to accept the consequences. But in the case of the title of this book, it's a truly sticky situation.

I grew up as the oldest daughter of two narcissistic parents. I was literally stuck between two people who were too emotionally immature to really understand how to raise children. As a child, I had no idea that my parents were narcissistic, and I didn't even know what that term meant! Life has been truly eye-opening, and I have learned so much about what my "normal" life really was and how it shaped who I am today.

When you read the title of this book, perhaps it caught your eye because you feel like this may describe your home life, or maybe you just wanted to see how in the hell this worked out.

Either way, I'm thrilled you picked it up and that you want to hear more of my story.

Some quick facts – I was raised in a solidly middle-class household in Northern Virginia. A "normal" family, if you will. If you're familiar with the area, I spent most of my life in Loudoun County, consistently ranked as one of the nation's wealthiest counties.

My parents were married in the fall of 1969 and stayed married for almost 25 years. Everyone thought my parents were amazing, and many of my friends told me they wished my mom were their mom. Both of my parents worked, and both were very successful in their careers. We had lovely homes, my sister and I each got a car at 16, and we received gifts and all the things that would describe us as very lucky. I went on vacation, and I don't remember wanting for much, but at the same time, not being overly spoiled. We were a sweet family of four. We fit all together at a 4-top restaurant table, so it was easy to get seated. We had a dog and later cats, two kids, and two incomes. Looking at us from the outside, we were a typical family. It should have been idyllic.

But all of that is precisely my point. From the outside looking in, you'd probably ask me why in the world I am writing this book. How in the world could I call out two well-respected, seemingly wonderful people as narcissists and claim that there's anything wrong with me today?

I didn't fully understand what my parents were until my late forties. After the death of her second husband, my mother came to live with us, and it's like the veil of my childhood was lifted. When I really started paying attention to her behavior, I realized not only did she have narcissistic traits, but that she probably had all of my life. And looking at my father, I realized he seemed to share so many of her behaviors as well.

I've since done a ton of research and found lots of books about a narcissistic mother OR a narcissistic father, but only a few books on having two narcissistic parents. Without an official diagnosis, I firmly believe both of my parents are narcissistic. They took turns feeding off of each other, and they damaged my sister and me in ways that I am still discovering. Do I think they had malicious intent? No, I do not. I believe that both of my parents are products of their own environments.

They grew up in the 50s and 60s during a time when therapy wasn't a thing, and as long as you looked like everything was fine, it was. Having a word that I could research was oddly satisfying. It was strange to read things online that described my childhood, and I found myself stunned at how often I was nodding my head while reading along.

Reading about narcissism, I found that there are mainly two types: Overt (or Grandiose) and Covert (or Vulnerable). Generally, I learned that the Overt narcissist likes power and control, and seems to show a lack of empathy for others, and is usually more interested in talking about themselves or their experiences. To me, this describes my father. Please note, I'm paraphrasing from lots of different sources I've read, so this is in no way official information. I'm just a girl who's gone through it and tried to make sense! The Covert kind usually has a high level of shame or inferiority combined with a feeling that they are misunderstood or not appreciated enough. They tend to react dramatically to criticism and can be very anxious while overthinking everything. For me, this describes my mother.

There are then additional traits that identify the narcissist that further describe things I've seen in my parents. Antagonistic is when the person can be competitive and willing to take advantage of people or a situation to help themselves. Very argumentative when they are proving they're right and very unwilling to listen to someone else's way of thinking. They have a need to show off and be seen. Here I see my father. My dad belonged to the country club, he drove snazzy cars, and he was very generous when it got him attention.

A Communal narcissist is someone who likes to be seen as generous and so helpful to others. This type looks for ways to show their support…volunteering, sponsoring, just basically being there without fail, while waiting to be recognized for their good deeds. This is my mother. She was a Girl Scout leader, a youth leader at church, and a pillar of her office during her career. Everyone loved and cherished her.

I'm the type of person who likes to try to understand how we got to this point, so please remember that this is just me making guesses. My father is the third of four boys. For many years, he was the youngest until his much younger brother was born. It seems that he may have been shown a lot of attention until he wasn't the baby anymore.

At that point, he had to try to get attention any way he could, and to me it feels like that's when these narcissistic traits began. His mother wasn't overly loving and was probably overwhelmed with all her sons, while his father was running multiple small businesses, tending a garden, and generally supporting the family.

My grandfather was a gentle man, and my grandmother was more domineering. I think that these experiences with his own parents were what turned into narcissism in my dad. I don't remember being told any stories about real abuse or neglect, but I know my grandmother didn't hesitate to take a hairbrush to the boys if they needed it.

On my mother's side, things were different. Her father was in the Navy, her mother was an executive assistant in Washington, DC, for a high-ranking government executive. She is the youngest of two children, and her brother was a lot like my dad, only much worse. My uncle wanted everyone to see and hear him, and he was never satisfied. I've heard many stories about pranks he played on my mother because they were often home alone while both parents were working. I'm very sure he caused her anxious nature, and that her way of coping was to be a constant good girl. She wanted everyone to recognize her goodness to counteract his badness.

The lives my parents lived before meeting each other shaped who they were as humans. While it's rare that two narcissists gravitate towards each other, I believe that they really didn't/don't know what they are and therefore didn't know enough to see that their relationship wouldn't work well long term. Plus, they were young when they met, I believe it was the end of their senior year of high school or the summer after, and they were probably around 18.

They got married at 20, and in case you don't know, you really might not be emotionally mature enough at that age to tie yourself to another human successfully! Spoiler alert, I went ahead and did the same thing myself, so I'm REALLY sure this might not be a good idea. We can all think of that one couple who fell in love as teens and stayed together for life, but in my opinion, that's the exception, not the norm.

When researching to write this book, I wanted to have facts that would help if you're starting the journey to try to figure out if you're the child of narcissistic parents. The items I've listed below are things commonly seen in a narcissistic parent, either mom or dad. I call it my narcissistic parent laundry list…

- Self-centered, needs admiration (although the dad may look for this outside the family more often), lacks empathy for the children, struggles to understand or share the children's feelings.

- Changes or denies events or uses guilt or manipulation to get what they want.

- Lack of boundaries and, further, no concern for teaching these children how to have their own boundaries.

- Loves to criticize others and their children but can't handle any criticism of their own. For the mom, this usually makes her become a victim, while the dad craves control over situations and people.

- The mom might try to compete with her children or use them as an extension of herself to have experiences through their accomplishments.

- The dad might seem one way to people outside the home and totally different at home, which can be confusing to the children.

- Finally, there's usually a favorite child and a scapegoat if there's more than one. This causes separation among those siblings so that she's always the most important.

Another list I built when looking into having both a narcissistic dad and mom was the common effects of spending your childhood in a home with two narcissistic parents. So many of these things I've dealt with throughout my life. It's always a little unbelievable when the information sought is so validating, but it's also a little sad to see your experiences listed out!

- Because of the need to prioritize their own needs, it's hard when no one is prioritizing the kids. It can be very unpredictable trying to figure out whose needs are more important in that moment, and the child never understands why their needs never make the top of the list.

- The amount of criticism that can be heaped upon a child with two narcissistic parents can be huge. Each parent is manipulating the child, and this results in a child who feels worthless or like they're never enough.

- These kids have no skills for setting boundaries, and if they try, the parents run right over them without care. This leads to difficulties in the future as well because not knowing how to set boundaries could lead to falling for a narcissistic partner.

- Spending a childhood serving the parents can cause the child to lose touch with who they are and have significant identity and self-esteem issues. Mental health concerns like anxiety, depression, people-pleasing tendencies, and post-traumatic stress are widespread.

When I get into my personal story, I'll point out the ways that I was impacted by so many of these traits. And how being stuck in the middle, as the child of two narcissistic parents, was an experience unlike any other. Living it, I had no idea what I was going through or why it was so impactful, but doing the research has given me so many ah-ha moments!

It feels redundant to mention it again, but my background isn't in the diagnosis of mental health disorders. I only know what I've read and experienced. Suppose any of what I've said resonates with you. I'm genuinely sorry. It's hard to live what others see as a picture-perfect upbringing and carry around oversized baggage. I've struggled to understand that trauma is defined by the person going through it.

My trauma is traumatic by my definition. Someone else might have had worse, or view my experiences as minor in comparison. But what I've lived through are my experiences and how they've affected me is my story to tell. And I'm choosing to tell it in the hopes that it does seem familiar to someone else. To let you know that maybe it's ok to be affected by a life that appears excellent on paper.

To see that having two emotionally immature parents that you might not want to stay in contact with doesn't make you evil. It makes you human. It makes you strong for finally picking yourself. And it makes you someone who has so much value. If you're still with me, buckle up and try not to gawk too much as you read the rest of this book. My life is like a sitcom. Welcome to episode 1!

Episode 1:
What Made Me, Me

I am the oldest of two children. My parents had me three years after they got married, in August of 1972. We lived in apartments until my grandparents sold my parents their single-family home sometime before I went to kindergarten.

I've been told they sold it to them for under market value and basically gave them that solid financial start as a generous gift. My sister was born in 1976, and I have seen many pictures of us as kids…we were cute, little blond girls in 1970s outfits that, of course, make me cringe today!

If I look back at my life, I'm not sure if my "memories" are really things that I remember or things I was told and pictures I have seen. For instance, I know I went to Disney World as a child, but I have no memory of actually being there. My mind's eye sometimes sees things that actually happened, and sometimes it sees a printed picture or knows a story about something that happened, but I can't quite put myself into that situation.

For instance, I can see a picture of my sister and me in matching dresses on the front walkway of our house, looking happy, but I cannot remember actually being there or feeling any happiness in that moment. I looked like I was enjoying the day, but I couldn't really tell you now if that was the case. I don't remember crying a ton. I know I wasn't beaten or starved. I do remember being on my own a lot, and I know I had an imaginary friend in pre-school. Her name was Jenny, and the only memory I have of her is my grandmother shutting her in the car door after picking me up one day, and me screaming while she thought I'd lost my mind and having no knowledge of who Jenny was!

So many of my memories revolve around my grandparents. My mom's parents were a massive part of my childhood, and thinking about it now, those memories are really real. I remember them trying to teach me to play tennis. I remember sledding with my grandfather and watching Redskins games with the sound down while listening to Sonny and Sam on the stereo.

I remember being fascinated by my grandmother's ability to type so fast while looking at me or actually holding a conversation too! I remember playing "games" with my grandfather that were actually life lessons…I was the manager of a hotel, and he was a disgruntled guest. I was a shop owner, he was a shopper, and I had to make change. I was the teacher, and he was a student, and I had to show him how to do math problems or understand a concept. They lived near us for so many years, and I walked home to their house from my elementary school every day.

My grandmother knew how to make all the dishes come out warm and on time with a single oven. She taught me how to set the table for a formal meal, and she showed me which purse went with what outfit and when it was acceptable to wear white.

She had a chaise lounge in her room, and it was my favorite place to read a book or talk on the phone as I got older. I can almost feel the comfort of that chair and the light smell of her perfume in her room. I can see so many details of their house and what the rooms look like. I know these memories are real and not just pictures I've been shown. I have a profound sense of safety when I think of all the time I spent with my grandparents, and I remember that when my grandmother said something, people listened, including my parents.

As a child, I don't remember thinking that my grandparents were better than my parents, but I don't think I really took the time to understand the differences between the two fully. I have to believe it's because my grandparents never did anything to make my parents look bad. They just made life better. They never talked about anything that was lacking; they just gave more, so we didn't really have cause to question. And knowing what I know now, these are the people who taught me the fundamental life lessons that I use to this day. Not my parents.

My sister told me a story about my grandmother pointing out to my mother that it might be time to potty train her because she "seemed to disappear when the need arose".

At the time, my mother looked dubious and stated that she'd figure it out on her own. I'm not sure who told that story to my sister, but it doesn't seem so crazy when you add to that the fact that I learned about the potty from our next-door neighbor when she trained her son. As a mom and grandma myself, I've taught or helped teach all of them to use the potty successfully, and I don't understand how you'd think it would be ok just to let it happen or let someone else do it!?

With the knowledge I've gained in the last 5 years, I now understand that my grandparents lived so close to us for most of our early lives so that they could help my parents raise their daughters. I've been told that my grandma didn't like my father, but I now firmly believe that my grandma knew her daughter and son-in-law weren't capable of being good parents, and they stuck around to make sure we got all the foundation we'd need for life. My grandma passed in 1992.

What I wouldn't give to be able to have a conversation with her now and ask her if all these things I'm thinking might make sense. I'd love for my grandmother to meet my kids and my husband and to see who I turned out to be. I'd love for both of them to get to see that so many of the things they taught me have stayed with me through my life, and I've built upon them to become who I am today.

I am very proud of who I am, and I believe they'd both be proud as well. I'd love to tell them that the love they shared with me as a child means so much to me for reasons I didn't understand then. I'd love for her to see my grandchildren and to see that I'm trying so hard to be for them what she was for me. I've always wanted to be like my grandma, and I genuinely believe I've given my children and grandchildren the best of what these two amazing humans taught me. So far, we have five amazing grandchildren, and they are everything!

Chapter One:
Childhood And the School Years

I have sporadic memories from my childhood. And as I mentioned earlier, I'm not sure what's a memory and what's a story or a picture I've seen of my life. I remember our house in Springfield, VA, where my elementary school was across the street. I remember my neighbors, Wanda and her son Kevin, of potty-training fame, and the family of six feral children that lived down the hill, who seemed to have the best family dynamic, even though it was constant chaos.

I remember my babysitter and how my mother got mad that she'd take us on errands around the beltway when she thought we were at the house. I remember my first-grade teacher's name, but I don't know anything about that first elementary school other than the image of the front of the school and her name.

I know that house had a gigantic willow tree in the backyard, and I know that my wooden playhouse got covered in cicada bodies one year. I remember getting the chicken pox. I remember my sister falling over the step to our family room and biting through her tongue while we were with a babysitter. I remember my sister falling out of the cart at the grocery store, and my mom and I following the ambulance to the hospital while I wailed that my sister was dead.

I have been told that I also fell out of the grocery cart as a toddler, and I find no surprise in the fact that my mother was there both times her children fell! I have seen plenty of pictures of us at birthday parties in the house and Christmases and things, and I feel like my expression is always unsure. Like I wasn't totally happy or totally sad...just like this little lost expression. Suppose you're saying to yourself, well, of course, same friend, same. I probably felt lost a lot of the time when my grandparents weren't around to make it make sense.

What I don't remember are day-to-day feelings about my life. I don't recall wishing my parents were anything other than what they were, because I don't think I saw that as an option. I guess somehow,

I just understood I was stuck with these people, and that was just the way it was. Like, I don't have a memory I can point to where I can say I was depressed or sad about my situation. I think that I told myself I wasn't abused, and I had a good home, so everything must be OK. There were so many kids worse off than me, so who was I to complain?

Both of my parents had good jobs. My mother worked for the federal government and my father for a government contractor. Here in the Washington metro area, these jobs are prevalent, but both of them were in management, and both were very respected by their colleagues.

They had friends they dined out with, and I remember parties held at our house for different occasions throughout the year. My mom's friends seemed to come and go for the most part…not too many that were there all the time. My dad has lasting friendships still today, and they're all in their 70s.

My dad was very gruff at home. Not overly talkative to my friends or to my sister and me. I have always just thought he was an asshole. He didn't pretend to be anything other than himself, and even when he was in the same room, he might not "BE" there. I remember getting hugs if I initiated them, and I love you never comes from him first.

If I say I love him, he'll say Love you too, but to have him say it without prompting doesn't happen often. When it does, it's a bit shocking! My sister and I learned to call him by his first name to get his attention. It was like you'd get 15 seconds to get out what you needed if you skipped calling him Pop!

My dad had a standing golf night with his friends every week, and he frequently went out for happy hour on Friday afternoons. I can remember joining him at the bar near his work and being paid a lot of attention by his friends when my sister and I were little. It always seemed really cool to be important in my dad's eyes during that time. But looking back, it was a show. I was there so that my dad's work friends could see his cute little girls and great family.

My sister and I knew that we were to behave in public and in front of others. We were taught to look adults in the eye, speak up with appropriate answers to questions, and not really act like kids. There is a funny memory of being out to eat at a pizza restaurant, and my sister and I were acting up. He stated rudely, "You're acting like kids". Well, of course we were!! When he found something, he enjoyed it; he needed to own all of it. For instance, he had the best golf clubs, he went to golf lessons, and he joined the country club with his friends. He bought new cars pretty often, and we moved houses three times in my life, and each one was bigger and in a better neighborhood.

He went through a phase of working on cars and bought all new tools. We had a computer and a microwave when they first came out, and he always made sure that the outside world would believe we were perfect. All of this I now know was because he needed admiration from others in order to feel secure. He wasn't one you went to with problems, and I don't ever recall him being involved in school stuff to any memorable extent. He was a good provider, and he seemed to love my mother, but who knows what I never saw. They eventually ended up divorcing.

My mom was more loving, it seemed, but now that I'm looking back with open eyes, I'm not sure that was really the case. She did the things moms were supposed to do. She fixed breakfast for us, even though I'm not really a breakfast person and would have preferred something light; she insisted on a full breakfast prepared by her. And if we didn't eat it or like it, it was a huge deal; obviously, we should have appreciated that she took the time. It's like there was some manual that said, "good moms feed their children breakfast," so she did, and being "good" children, we should eat it and thank her for it.

As a mom myself, I provided plenty of breakfast choices for my kids and assisted as needed, but if they wanted a granola bar vs a waffle, who was I to care? And dinners…most of the time, my mom cooked dinner while sipping on amaretto out of a fancy cordial glass. She collected them for a while and had so many to choose from. I have no idea how much she drank, and I don't remember her being drunk, but I do remember it being a normal thing to see her standing by the stove in the kitchen with a glass in hand. Dinner was served at the table, and we ate together almost every night unless my dad was playing golf.

They would discuss their day and work stuff, and mostly my sister and I just sat there. She is three years younger than I am, so I remember her talking more than I did, but I also know my goal was to fly under the radar. I didn't do much to get attention. Grades were fine, friends were fine, and I did what I should because it was easier than having them focus their attention on me. I have this wacky mental picture of a grid, and in the image, there's trouble when something pops up over the grid. Like a flag…when the flag pops up, it's something to pay attention to, and that's not the goal. Therefore, picture me under the grid just hanging out and living life and never poking my flag up for anyone to see. That was how I strived to live. As long as I played the part and did what was expected of me, no one paid attention.

During elementary school, my mom got my sister and me involved in the local theater. My sister has a gorgeous singing voice and got the lead in numerous plays both as a child and later as an adult. My mom made me audition as well, and I was always given a role in the children's chorus of the play. My sister loved it, and my mom loved the attention. She and my father got involved in the backstage side of the theater company, and eventually so did I. This experience gave my mother the opportunity to live vicariously through my sister.

Our family became part of both the acting side because of my sister and the show production side because of my parents. We were involved in this for many years, honestly, until I was old enough to drive and could get away from being involved. My mother was the doting stage mother, and everyone heaped praise on her and my father. My sister has told me later that she always felt like their little performer, and not in a good way. I can remember so many situations where they made her sing on demand for their friends or in public.

I now know that I was the favored child in that neither of my parents overstepped boundaries with me to a considerable extent. They didn't overshare their relationship with me, as I've been told they did with my sister. I was usually just left alone, or that's what I remember. I don't know if that's because I was the oldest or because I was less willing to listen. Or it could be that because I was so busy staying under my grid, I wasn't fascinating to either of them. I wasn't the best or the worst, and for that reason, maybe I wasn't anything to worry about. By the time I was in middle school, my grandparents had moved down to Florida, and I remember staying by myself a ton. At the time, I think I really was thankful to be left alone and kept out of the spotlight. It was a relief not to need to be part of their show.

But being alone also left me with a lot of time to think about my own thoughts. I had a tough time with my sense of self, and being part of that constant pretend-perfect family was exhausting and did nothing to build that understanding of who I was. I imagine at the time I had very intense feelings about what I was experiencing, as a teen who wouldn't, but at this point in my life, I have no memory of that. It is said that adults who have very few memories of childhood most likely blocked them to hide what was traumatic.

When you spend so much of your time on edge or watching what's going on around you, the part of your brain tasked with making memories doesn't work. Writing this book brought back so many things that I had to uncover about my life, and I'm honestly not sure I want to dig down too deep. At fifty-three, do I really need to remember how sad I was at twelve? How would that serve me well at this point?

Two distinct instances stand out to me as pivotal in my struggle with self-esteem, though. One happened in middle school with my mother. There was a boy I liked once, I can't even remember his name, but I can see his adorable face in my mind. Behind our house, there was an open fielded area between our neighborhood and the tiny strip mall in our community.

The boys would ride their BMX bikes around the hills of dirt. Pretty sure the dirt mounds were leftover dirt from the building of our section of homes. And it made a great dirt bike hangout for middle school-aged kids. I had so much space in our community to walk with friends to the pool, around the pond, to the High's convenience store. It was on one of those walks that my friends and I passed by this boy and his friends.

We stopped to chat and flirt, and this amazing boy, whom I was crushing on so hard, HUGGED me goodbye! I was DYING! Later that night, I was telling my mom all about this experience, and I remember she just looked at me with a lack of expression and said to me that the only reason boys hug girls is that they want to feel their boobs. And that I needed to keep that in mind and not just hug any boy that initiates it because it didn't mean he liked me.

To this day, I can feel the feelings I felt at that moment. Feeling like he couldn't possibly like me and that he just wanted a quick feel. It hurt my heart. I don't remember anything about that boy after that. I don't recall if I still crushed on him, but just that I had learned that my body was just something to interest boys, not that I was someone to like. I, of course, went on to date boys and get married, but that comment has stuck with me, and it's something I've had to rewire my brain not to believe.

Narcissistic parents also train their children to believe that their needs and wants are the most important. They don't want their children to rely on each other, but instead only rely on that narcissistic parent.

In my experience growing up with two narcissists, my parents liked to each take a child and keep that child tethered to them, feeling responsible for their happiness. I always chose my father. When we shopped for holiday gifts, we'd all go to the mall, my dad and I would shop while my mom and sister did as well. We'd each have a list of gifts to get, and we'd only meet back up when it was time to leave.

My sister was always with my mom, and if my dad weren't around, I'd be by myself usually. I'm not sure if this was because my mom needed my sister's attention all to herself or because I was the moody older sister, and it was easier to let me stay home, but either way, I wasn't as exposed to my mother as I was to my father.

I have a couple of pivotal memories from my teen years that hurt to think about. Leading up to my 16th birthday, my parents had been talking to me about driving and getting a car. On my birthday, my dad handed me a box that contained a set of keys…to their vehicles. He told me I wasn't ready to have the freedom of my own car, but if they weren't using theirs, I'd have my own set of keys. Sigh. Soon after, I did end up getting a vehicle, but I'd asked for a cute Toyota pick-up and received an old bench seat Dodge RAM pick-up…basically the Pinto of pick-ups. Side note here, my sister received a newer Ford Mustang as her first car. It was beautiful.

Another standout memory involved my mother and birth control. I'd been dating the same boy for about a year and quietly had a pregnancy scare that I told no one about. My friend convinced me I needed to ask my mom to take me to the gyno to get on the pill. I finally did it, and she spent the next week flopping back and forth from being mad at me to being supportive. She finally made the appointment, took me to the doctor, and then didn't speak to me for two days after. She insisted I wasn't ready to have sex, and she couldn't believe I was considering it. I remember wishing I'd gone to Planned Parenthood and left her out of it altogether.

The worst memory I have from high school was the death of my grandfather the morning of my senior prom, May 12, 1990. He and my grandmother had been such a force for good in my life, and he was suddenly gone. They'd been living in Florida for a few years, and I spoke and wrote to them pretty often.

One of the last letters I got from my grandfather warned me to really think about my high school boyfriend and whether he was someone I wanted to tie myself to forever. He reminded me that I had so much potential and that a high school dropout wasn't really a good choice. I have wished so many times over the years that I could sit down with my grandfather one more time and let him know that while it took a bit for my decision-making to get better, it did finally.

Chapter Two:
Getting Married and Divorced

After high school, I went to college for two years. Looking back, we all agreed that I wasn't ready to go so soon after losing my grandfather. But for years, I'd been told that you went to college after high school. I looked at three schools, and the one school that my mom had attended for a year invited me to accept attendance at my tour. So, I did. It seemed easy just to say yes, and of course, my mother was thrilled.

The school was about 6 hours from home, and that felt like an opportunity as well. I spent my first semester of school dating that high school boyfriend. We broke up during Christmas break, and he spent the second semester trying to talk me back into a relationship with him. Over summer break, we rekindled somewhat, but not really. First and second semesters, my grades were good, then a little less, but totally on par for freshman year, and my history with school in general. Third semester, I partied a lot more and went to a lot fewer classes.

The GPA began to tank, and my heart just wasn't in it. When I returned for Christmas break that second year, my grandmother passed away on January 5, 1992. Her death was so brutal. She passed while we were all out, and she was home alone. At her funeral, the minister commented on her dying alone…I believe he followed that up with something about her having God with her and not really being alone, but the first part of his comment almost made me stand to argue with him in front of the funeral attendees.

But of course, pretending to be the perfect child prevented me from expressing myself in such a public manner. My parents decided that sending me back to school just a week or so after her death was the best thing to do. Spoiler, it wasn't. I drank and partied the entire semester, and my grades were horrendous. The school invited me to take time off to figure out if college was really my thing when they suspended me for my low GPA!

In the summer of 1992, I went to work for the US Park Service as an admin, and I lived at home to start. A friend introduced me to the man who would become my first husband. I'd known him for years as he was enrolled for a time at my high school. He didn't attend really, but at 16 chose to quit school to work. There were SO MANY RED FLAGS with this man and this relationship, but at the time, I had no idea how to look for those, and he seemed like a great project boyfriend. He was rough around the edges, and I was the perfect girl to smooth him out.

He had a pretty decent drug and alcohol problem (red flag), but while dating me, I got him down to just pot and mostly beer, so that's, of course, an indication that I was so good for him! My mother refused to let me spend the night at his apartment, even though I was 20 years old that year and had been making my own sleeping decisions while away at school for the last two years.

To get away from her rules, my friend and I decided to get an apartment together. She and I had known each other since middle school, and we both had grand visions of living like the cast of Friends in our own place! Unfortunately, we both brought boyfriends with us to that apartment, and we never got that magic roommate living experience. My boyfriend was controlling and slowly pulled me away from my friends, so I was heavily reliant on him and his friends.

He asked me to marry him during that year of living in the apartment, and we were married in September of 1993. If you're doing the math, that's just about a year of dating/engagement, and I married him the month after I turned 21.

The longer we were together, the more emotionally abusive he became. I was never good enough, or skinny enough, or quiet enough, or just basically enough. I don't really remember my parents reacting in any specific way when we announced we were engaged. My mother was involved in planning our wedding, but really it was a big party full of my parents' friends where we happened to get married. I remember the reception venue had a balcony area where the 15-20 people our age stayed while all of my parents' friends and the central part of the reception were down on the main floor.

And something that really should have been a red flag indicator for me was that my first husband put no friends on his side of the wedding party. He had his brothers and this stepfather stand up for him. Not a single guy that he was close enough to was included.

I'd love to say that my marriage wasn't all bad, but honestly, it was. I was constantly on edge because now I was supposed to keep this man happy while still trying to keep my parents happy as well. He was a menace, though. Constantly in an argument with someone. At work, with his family, and with random strangers at a bar. There wasn't a lot of peace, but I think I was so used to that in my life that I didn't know how to push back. In the '80s, there used to be all these after-school specials that taught you about different topics. I distinctly remember one that told girls if your boyfriend hits you, it's not ok. That's abuse, and you need to get away.

My ex never hit me. But he abused me in so many other ways that the damn special never talked about. He questioned everything I did; hence, I never felt confident in any decision I made for myself. He called me names...fat, stupid, lame...usually these were said as a "joke", but they take a toll anyway. And please let me explain, I was a size four at this time in my life. I was anything but fat. If I sat on his lap, he'd pretend I was breaking his leg, and he'd laugh and push me off. It was always in front of other people, too, and with my training, I'd just laugh it off and pretend everything was fine. This is all emotional abuse. Husbands and parents aren't supposed to make you question yourself or feel bad. People who love you should raise you up! I was so low when I met him that I just allowed this to happen day after day, and looking back, it makes me so sad for that girl. She should have known she deserved better.

My parents divorced during my first marriage in 1995. It was a dramatic mess! My parents announced the separation while driving my ex and me to the airport. We were leaving for a 10-day Bahamas vacation, and the four of us were alone in the car when they dropped the news. I spent most of that vacation on the phone with one of them or my sister. During their divorce process, I ended up taking care of my father's life. I paid his bills, went to a settlement on two homes, picked him up after an involuntary stay at the ER for a psych evaluation, and listened to him bitch and moan constantly. One moment was a glimpse at the future me who is able to stand up to her parents.

My ex and I were out to dinner with a large group of friends. My phone kept ringing and pinging, and my ex insisted I go outside and take care of it to stop interrupting his dinner. Standing in front of the restaurant, my father told me for the 100th time that he was going to kill himself. I snapped and told him not to fuck it up. There was a long, quiet pause, then he asked me to repeat myself. I again told him not to fuck it up. If he was going to kill himself, he needed to do it right and not end up a vegetable for me to take care of. After that, he started to laugh and told me to enjoy the rest of my evening. Thankfully, that was the last time he mentioned suicide.

My ex and I were married from 1993 to 1998, and in October 1996, we welcomed our beautiful little daughter. Becoming a mother changed me. In my mind, I now had this tiny being that entirely depended on me for existence. My now ex wasn't overly involved in the pregnancy or in being a dad. Thus, I took over, and I owned that damn thing! I began to get stronger and stand up more, and that is when our marriage took a back seat.

We argued more often, and he went out with friends a lot more than before. We all know how relationships like this end! It turns out he was cheating the entire time, but since I was at home being a mom, I had no idea. He played so many games during our marriage. He'd delete messages from my family on our answering machine, or when I did get to hear them, he'd bitch to me the entire time, so I'd have to listen multiple times to hear the whole thing. He complained about my attention to our daughter and my choices for dinner.

He'd hold her for a little bit while I cooked, but always asked me what he should do with her when he was tired of being responsible for her. If you're noticing so many narcissistic traits in this man, you are exactly correct! At the time, I believed I went out and married a man like my father, but after my epiphany with my mother in my late 40s, I now know I married them both! He was self-centered and sought admiration from friends and girls in bars.

He had so few feelings about being a dad and having a daughter; therefore, he struggled to be involved. He manipulated me constantly, and I firmly believe that becoming a mom allowed me to see that he needed to be less important to me than she was. Our marriage came to an abrupt halt in October 1998 after our daughter's 2nd birthday party when he informed me, while drunk, that he no longer wanted to be married to me. Ultimately, I found out he'd already started a new relationship with our friend and neighbor across the street, and she'd given him the ultimatum to get out of his marriage, but I didn't figure that out until a few months after our split.

Looking back at that relationship, the fact that she decided she wanted him was truly a gift. I would have kept working on my marriage and trying to find a balance, but she let me out.

She didn't take my man; she took my problem!

Sadly, the reason she wanted him was that I painted such a good outward picture of what my world looked like that no one knew the truth. I was taught by my parents that the image you present to others about your home life is the most important thing.

You don't admit what it really looks like, so bless her heart, she believed every word and later told me that she was mad that I hadn't been honest about my marriage and that she was sorry she'd married him! I literally laughed out loud at that one! I was trained by two of the best narcissists I know and followed the rules while married to my narcissistic husband! I was the poster child for being under other people's control!!

Our divorce took almost 18 months. He was in a new relationship for 20+ months of that time! He fought me on anything and everything. He wanted the house and everything in it. His new girlfriend wanted custody of our daughter, and he wanted me to pay oodles of money. During this time, my parents really stepped up and helped my daughter and me. My dad paid for my attorney and my mom, and her new husband, let us stay with them until we found an apartment.

They also bought me a car that I then made payments on to them because my credit was destroyed when my ex left our townhouse, which he insisted on keeping, and let it go to foreclosure. He refused to sign a settlement agreement, and we had to take him to court to get the divorce finalized. It was complete misery, and during those 18 months, he took every opportunity to berate me for everything via text, phone calls, voice mails, and emails. In the end, I got full custody of our daughter, and I got to keep everything I took from the home when I moved out.

We both had legal fees, but thankfully, my dad paid for mine, and he just filed for bankruptcy on his own. I have been divorced from him for 25 years, and if given the right circumstances, my father will mention how I wouldn't have that divorce without him. Not once did he mention how sorry he was that my marriage was so detrimental to me as a human or how much it hurt him to see his daughter go through this. When my attorney wrote up the request for dissolution of our marriage, he put all of my dirty laundry on those pages.

When I read it, it took me a moment to realize that the words on those pages had really been my life for over five years with this man. It was a painful and broken story, and I know my dad read it too. But not once to this day has either he or my mom told me how sorry they are that I went through all of that. They rose to the occasion of helping me in order to be recognized for providing that help. I am thankful because the help they provided allowed me to move forward in life as a single mom and begin to find out who I really was, but here's the thing…they didn't do it for me; they did it for themselves. And if they hadn't raised me the way they did, I might never have married such a horrible human.

He's still around today and pops in and out of our daughter's life to wreak havoc as he sees fit. He's on wife number three, and at 53, he has an elementary-aged second daughter. His third wife is about 10 years younger than he is, probably because it's easier to fool a younger woman than it is those his age.

I feel sorry for her because I know the life she's living and how it's most likely going to turn out, and it's so crazy because, in a small way, I feel sorry for him. He's a narcissist and has no idea. His mother ruined him very early on, and he's never gone to therapy to fix any of his issues.

He has a limited relationship with our daughter and no relationship with his grandchildren. In my opinion, they are all better with his absence in their lives, but, sadly, he's missing out on some incredible people, and he'll continue to be broken, probably for the rest of his life.

Chapter Three:
Finding Me and Finding Him

While my divorce was ridiculously dramatic, I know I didn't miss my ex or our life. I missed my townhouse, which was so cute and decorated just the way I liked, but that's really it. Just days after leaving my marriage, I felt free. I was able to make any decision I wanted at any time, and as a young mom, that was amazing. I also used that time to pretend to be a single woman in my 20s every other weekend.

I went to bars and clubs; I had a few hookups, and I had a lot of fun. I wasn't interested in meeting anyone permanently, and I was very happy with my freedom. I lived in a cute little two-bedroom apartment, and I was in charge of my life. I ate when I wanted, I watched what I wanted on TV, and I learned just how incredibly capable I was in all kinds of ways. I became a strong woman! In my senior year of high school, I had this amazing English teacher who loved to shout, "*I am a woman, hear me roar*", and let me tell you, I was roaring! I also went to work hungover after ladies' night, and I more often than I'd like to admit didn't have enough money for cat food.

But we all made it! We spent a year in our first apartment, and my daughter went to daycare daily while I worked. It was a really cool learning experience about who I was, and even though I had to call the police twice on my ex and I had disastrous interactions with him weekly, I really had a chance to figure out who I was as a woman and what I was willing to accept in a future partner. At this point in my life, I think I was just living day-to-day.

I don't remember looking back at my marriage and feeling one way or another, just looking forward to what each new day brought. This was truly the first time I'd lived without any other adults in all of my life. I wasn't thinking about how other people wanted me to live, and I was just living the way I wanted. My memories of that year don't have much sadness in them. I enjoyed meeting new friends and going to new places, and even when I was truly "alone," it was more of a novelty than something to be sad about. I know that I tried to make my marriage work for close to five years with a man who wasn't doing the same. I know I put up with so much during my marriage that so many other women wouldn't have accepted. I wasn't ashamed, and I didn't have a lot of self-blame that my marriage was over.

He cheated, and they wanted to be together, which freed me from my old life and allowed me to create a new one. This wasn't a rebuilding of my life after divorce, but more of building a true life. For the first time, I built myself for myself without any other opinions. In what I believe is another example of the way I have managed trauma in my life, I put a lid on my marriage, and I started fresh with myself.

In the summer of 1999, a friend offered to introduce me to this guy she thought I'd really like. I told her, "No, thank you!" I dodged it for a few weeks and then finally hung out with her and her fiancé at a racetrack in Manassas, Va. We drank beers and laughed while people-watching in this truly redneck environment.

At the end of the race, I did end up meeting that guy, and here I am over 26 years later still with him. He is everything my parents and ex are not. He's kind and caring, he loves me unconditionally, and he lets me be me no matter what. He's loved me through the really ugly parts of our lives, and *he's my true best friend.*

There's a meme online about being a husband's girl...not a mom or daddy's girl, and that's me. I am a husband's girl. He's one of only three people who have ever loved all of me, the other two being my grandparents.

He tells me I'm beautiful even though I don't believe him, and he indulges me in so many ways. He kills all the bugs in the house, and he touches all the raw meat because that grosses me out. For extreme circumstances when he's not home, I do have my vacuum for the bugs and pink, rubber gloves for the meat, but he's happy to take care of all of that without complaint! When I met him, he didn't know how to do the laundry because his mom always took care of it for him, and he'd never had a serious relationship. He met me during my horrible divorce, and he never tried to be anything other than supportive.

Together, we have raised my daughter along with our two additional children, and we've done this with the belief that we're supposed to be in our children's lives and give them everything we never had.

The really cool thing about my husband is that he loves me. Period. *He just loves ME for me.* The happy parts, the sad parts, the weird things that randomly trigger me, my urges to take a moment, and everything in between. He loves me unconditionally. I honestly didn't understand that concept until I met him. We've had so many crazy things happen in our lives, and he just rides through them with me, and we figure it out together.

It is us against the world, always and forever!

Our son was diagnosed with Crohn's Disease in 2008, and I spent 10 days at the hospital with him in December. The night we finally came home, I pulled up our street and found our house completely lit up with Christmas lights. I love lights, and this man put them up, so it would be the first thing I saw when I came down the street. And along the line of lights…the first Christmas we were together was my first holiday in my own place, and we figured out I had grabbed my Christmas ornaments from my old life, but I had no lights. I was putting up the tree very late in the season, and he spent an hour going to different stores to get me lights for that damn tree. So hokey, but this man truly lights up my life!!

I'm not going to sit here and tell you our life has been all roses and sunshine. With three kids, that's almost impossible! But the thing about this relationship that I haven't had before is that we genuinely want the best for each other. Neither of us is out for ourselves, and that makes a relationship so much easier. We can be ourselves, and we cheer for each other constantly. We've both always worked, and we are excited for each career milestone we achieve. We share chores around the house, and he spent plenty of nights awake with a crying kid while I tried to catch some sleep.

When we do fight, I, of course, don't fight fair because I'm pretty damaged, but I've learned over the years that he wants the best for me, and he's just trying to communicate his feelings on whatever is happening. He's not trying to manipulate me or cause me harm, and once I figured that out, we've been able to talk about things vs fighting about them. Bless his heart, he took a lot of crap in the beginning! It's tough to be in a healthy relationship after so many years of unhealthy living.

Together, we believe that we are the parents we have been to our children because we wanted more as kids, so we gave it to them. He is and always has been all in with our lives. He has held everyone while they cried, he works hard at his career, and as the coach of everything, I've talked him into coaching for our kids. He's been a cheer dad, and he's weighed in on our daughters' outfit choices over the years with care and consideration for the women they needed to become.

He overcame the loss of his father when he was twelve, and I truly believe that the reason he and I fit so well is that we had a strong sense of ourselves when we met, and we've communicated well with one another on every topic. My kids will tell you that no one is allowed to come at me without him coming at them. They love to say that they all knew not to go too far when he was home because once you made him mad for going too far with mom, it was over, and you were faced with his never-ending lectures and his disappointment. They'd do almost anything to avoid that!

Looking back, I believe that I had healed myself from my first marriage and had dealt with my past. I was a happy and healthy working mom of three, I had a strong, healthy marriage, and together we were raising great kids. It was all golden, and I'd really pulled myself out of that ugly place and was ready to ride off into that empty nest sunset and enjoy those golden years. But...you know this book isn't over, so obviously that's not what happened!

Chapter Four:
The Beginning of the End

In July of 2014, we had been living in Gainesville, VA, for about 8 years. We made a move back to Loudoun County and into a home owned by my mother and her second husband. They had recently downsized to a townhouse, and their single-family, five-bedroom house wasn't selling for market prices in the condition it was in. Not that it was run down, but it hadn't been updated since the early 90s, and it wasn't going to sell for what they needed out of it. We had been renting and took the opportunity to move in and take over their mortgage payment. This provided us with more stability and a great project home to renovate.

The neighborhood had gorgeous mature trees and families with kids. We figured one day we'd all decide to sell it, and they agreed to provide us with a down payment for a new house at that time. My family and I tore out walls and flooring and renovated the entire basement and first floor. We loved the changes we made in the house, and I had a gorgeous kitchen with a massive island for everyone to gather around and a pantry large enough to hide in! It was glorious! We love DIY projects, and we enjoyed all of the work we put into the house.

Sadly, in November 2017, my mother's husband died after an eight-year battle with cancer. In 2018, she asked my husband and me if she could build on to the back of the house and move in with us. Since technically she owned the house, of course, we said yes. Plus, we all thought it would be a perfect way for her to live out her days right there with us, where we could assist as needed.

At this time, we had no idea of what was to come, and the knowledge I was going to gain by living with my mother again on a full-time basis. She and our kids hatched a plan to build a pool in the backyard as well, and now this beautiful home has really become a showplace where my kids could make unforgettable memories, and we could entertain friends and family as we wished. As part of all of this, she refinanced the house and put my husband on the deed. Now we were homeowners again. We split all the household bills, and I did all the cooking for the family.

We also renovated the master bedroom and bathroom, and I was able to design a phenomenal bathroom of my dreams! Soaking tub inside a huge glass shower enclosure, a dimmable chandelier, speakers for streaming, and a stackable washer and dryer, so I no longer had to share with my kids! This room and a bottle of wine could keep me busy for hours!! I loved that bathroom! All of this should have been perfection, but soon it wasn't.

But we started to notice things. My mother wasn't interested in cooking, but somehow had the expectation that I'd prepare her dinner at the appropriate time for her each day, even if our kids weren't home from after-school sports or work yet. She would be pretty pissed if we waited to eat once our children were home. She took to coming out of her area of the house and wandering through the kitchen to see if anything was being fixed. She never just asked when dinner would be ready, but instead just lurked around with a frown. And she frequently would insert herself smack in the middle of any gathering we chose to have at the house. Talking to our friends about us, even while we stood and listened.

It became exhausting to host our friends because we'd have to spend time explaining my mom. She even started to put herself or her chair between me and anyone we'd invited over to put herself right in the middle and pull attention away from me. It was bizarre! And if my husband and I sat in the living room watching TV into the night, we'd better call out to her that we were going to bed, or she'd shoot me a snarly text about how we must have forgotten! Another strange thing would happen if we decided to binge-watch TV on a random Saturday. My mother would wander by every hour or so to announce that she was just in her room reading or whatever, and she'd repeatedly ask if we had plans. She hated it when we did nothing, and it almost made us feel like we had to be doing something or at least out of her line of sight to be lazy. But when we did have a project we were working on, she'd tell my husband how I worked him too hard and never let him have any downtime!

In the beginning, we thought it would be most helpful to have her there in the house where we could keep an eye on her, but it became a situation where we were expected to be at her beck and call for any reason. She couldn't reach something, or she had a lightbulb out. She needed the time changed in her car or wanted to know our plans for the weekend. If we tried to leave the house without her, the guilt trip was severe.

This is all very typical behavior for a narcissist, but because I'd lived away from her for so long and only seen her in "event mode," I had completely forgotten what life with my mother was like. And every few months, she'd corner me to get me to convince her that she wasn't a burden and that we loved having her there. She'd push me into the position of defending her behaviors as ok and making her believe we were thrilled with her in every way.

It was so manipulative, and at the time, I knew what was happening and couldn't stop myself from telling her lies to make her feel like things were great. I would say anything to keep her happy, and I would walk away from the conversation feeling so disgusted with myself. I hate to lie. I try so hard in my personal life to never lie about anything. I am very truthful with my kids, and I go out of my way to stay away from situations that would need a lie to get through. Do I call in sick when I'm not? Of course, but I never blame it on anything other than myself, and I never elaborate with more information than necessary.

This is hard, though, because I have a minimal tolerance for other people who lie. And my definition of a lie is really slim. For instance, you're telling a story to a group of people, and I am part of that story. As you're telling it, you add some details that weren't in the original version…kinda spice up the details if you will. But in my head, alarm bells are going off. You're playing to the audience with this extraordinary story, but I'm looking for a place to run. I was involved in so many lies with my family and my ex that I am seriously traumatized when someone adds me to a less-than-truthful story now. And when I don't call you out in front of everyone (because that would be horrible for both of us), I feel that old familiar feeling of disgust, and it kills me. I've talked to my therapist about this, and she helped me see that the issue is mine. At times, people spice up a story for a variety of reasons, and as long as the story doesn't hurt me in the way it's being told, I probably need to take a second to think before I cut off friends like I'm the mafia!

Growing up with emotionally immature parents who either lied or didn't stop the other from lying, and a spouse who lied, really did a number on me. I kinda have trust issues, but in a weird way. Like I trust you until I don't, and when I don't, it takes forever (if ever) to win back my trust. I need blatant honesty even if it hurts. Something my parents will never understand.

Chapter Five:
Going No Contact

About the last year and a half of my mother living with us, things really started to take a turn. We had weathered COVID, and by this time, we had three beautiful grandchildren. My daughter and the kids lived in our basement, and I started to notice odd behavior from my mother when she interacted with the kids. She'd often pull one into her suite and baby gate the others out. I wasn't always the same kid, but it was the same outcome.

The left-out kids always felt hurt and wanted to be part of what was going on in her room. One really memorable moment happened when I was in the kitchen and overheard her talking to them. The back of the house was one big open concept space from the kitchen in the far left to the family room on the far right. I could stand at my island and see all the way to the windows on the opposite end of the house. I was cooking dinner, and the kids had been playing in the family room. I didn't hear the words being said, but I heard the tone of my mother's voice. It literally chilled me.

I whipped around and loudly asked what was going on. She looked from them to me with a complete chameleon change in her facial expression. She had been giving them a horrible look and tone, and when she turned to me, the veil dropped, and she smiled and told me nothing was wrong at all! Instantly, I remembered what that tone and face meant, and I went into protector mode. I walked in there and took all three kids away from her. These babies were probably six, three, and two at the time, and there was nothing they could be doing that warranted her behavior! I vowed at that moment to never allow her to be alone with my grandchildren again.

During this time, I worked from home for a local government contractor. It got to the point that to have quiet time with my husband at the end of the day, I'd hide upstairs in my office until after he got home. Once we went downstairs, we had to share life with my mom. And my mother is also better when she has a man in her life. Living with us, she was alone and had no male focus, so the girls and I started to notice she'd gravitate towards my husband and son. They were the first people she looked to for approval, and she'd frequently double-check my thoughts with my husband's once she could get him alone. It was infuriating. I am a very successful career woman; I have a master's degree, and I've raised three children. She asked me my thoughts and opinions, but would only act on them if my husband agreed. We got wise to her ways, though, and when she'd hit him with things in the evenings, he'd look at her and ask what I had said before he answered her.

She hated that! She'd grudgingly tell him what I'd said, and he'd usually follow it up with "sounds like a good plan" or something like that, and she'd profusely thank him for his thoughts. She also began to answer every question or thought he had at dinner. I could never inject my thoughts until she'd interjected hers first. It was like she wanted to compete with me for his attention. Once I saw it, I stopped interacting with her. I was the one married to this man, and I'm not about to compete with my mother for his attention. Thankfully, he and I have a good relationship, and we'd talk about these things and devise plans for handling her actions.

The end came after a few months of awful interactions. She'd been behaving poorly through the holidays, and everything was coming to a head. She and I had a huge fight in her suite, and she suggested that we sell the house and all go our separate ways. Usually, it was at this point that my training would kick in and I'd convince her that I needed her, and I'd talk her down. This happened so many times over the six years we all lived together, but this time I didn't. I told her that sounded like a great idea and that I'd call the realtor! This was in February, and by May, the house had sold.

She moved into an apartment, and we stayed in the house until after my youngest had graduated from high school. We moved about 30 minutes away from where she was living, and we moved on. It was devastating to leave the house I expected to stay in forever, the house that we'd worked so hard to renovate and that had poured so much of my heart into it. But that's just a place, and when you take your people with you, there can always be another place.

At closing for the house, the proceeds from the sale were split 50/50 between my husband, me, and my mother. Our realtor was a friend of mine, and she ensured that we got the most for the house and that we didn't close at the same time as my mother. When my mother attended the closing, she asked our realtor if she had to share the escrow money with us?! Because the mortgage stayed in her name only when she added my husband to the deed, and because in the settlement agreement we all signed, I didn't think to mention the escrow account, that decision was hers to make, and she chose to keep it to herself. She also never contributed to the $8,000 we spent to repaint the house, do some landscaping, and general prep for sale tasks. I hated having to spend the money, but it was all worth it to get out of our current living situation.

I don't think there was a single defining moment when I emotionally detached from my mother. I think it was a gradual process where I slowly let go of the behavior expectations, and I started doing what I wanted. I can be a petty person at times, and I think I finally started letting that person make the decisions when it came to how I dealt with my mom. For instance, I stopped saying good night and responding to her snarky texts.

As a woman in my 40s, I don't have to tell my mom I'm going to bed. It might seem ridiculous, but it was a tiny step toward living my way and not just doing what was expected. I have often referred to myself as the family admin because both of my parents would have me make reservations, plans, or organize things. I stopped doing that, too, for both of them during this period. I stopped coming to their rescue. I felt an insane amount of guilt for putting a stop to the things I'd always done, but I also felt so relieved. I didn't have to prioritize their happiness, and further, I didn't have to let their unhappiness bother me. This was a choice I was free to make for myself. To this day, I have to tell myself that this is still ok. The amount of rewiring I've had to do to teach myself to release that guilt is immense. But guilt doesn't serve anyone but the guilt-er. If I, or you, do things because you feel guilty, you're not serving yourself, and you won't gain true happiness from your actions. This might be a daily reminder or affirmation that you need to adopt, but the more you stop giving in to guilt, the more emotionally healthy you'll become.

Episode II:
What Now?

Moving out of that house in 2023 gave me the out I needed to let go. Much like the neighbor girl let me out of my icky marriage, the sale of that house let me walk away from my responsibilities as a daughter of narcissists. I am making my own decisions on how I want to behave, and I'm responsible for my own happiness. I have peace in my life because I decided to put myself first. It has been so scary and liberating. That summer, we bought a new house in a town further west in Loudoun than I've ever lived. My youngest daughter started her first year of college, and my older two were living their own lives as well.

Our granddaughter moved in with us, and we began life as a three-person household. On weekdays, my husband went to work, my granddaughter to school, and the dogs and I spent the day working in a quiet house. I no longer had to hide in my office, and I could greet my husband at the door or anywhere else I wanted. We had conversations just the two of us, and we sat on the couch for an entire day if we felt like it.

I feel like it might have been my first experience of peace. There were many aspects of the house that I missed, but the peace I felt in that moment was worth the loss. To be honest, that's what it was. I had lost a home I'd put so much of myself into, but I'd gained so much of myself by leaving it. It took some time to turn that thinking around. For sure, it wasn't overnight, but the more days of peace that I put behind me, the more at peace I am with my decisions.

I have limited contact with my dad. We used to stay with him over Thanksgiving, but he was always very anxious when my family was in town, and usually by day three, the complaints were significant, so we spent more time away from him than we did with him. I can't understand why he wouldn't want to spend time with his grandchildren. For a few years after that, we'd stay locally, and all go over on Thanksgiving Day to make a big family meal. Still, two years ago, he made such an ass of himself and treated me so poorly that my youngest daughter told him the only thing she'd remember about him when he was gone was that he was an asshole. That child isn't afraid to call people out on their behavior and is someone I am so proud to know.

Last year, we met for dinner at a restaurant, and I stopped by his house for about an hour while we were in town. I live eight hours away from my father, and we're down to seeing each other for less than 4 hours when I'm in town. We text or message a few times a month and talk on the phone maybe once a month. He's not overly interested in hearing about what we have going on unless it's got a drama component, and he can criticize the way we've handled things.

Over the years, he's tried to tell me to correct my adult children for choices he feels they've made that are wrong, and I've used my newfound boundaries to tell him to feel free to reach out directly if he has something he'd like them to know. He's really not interested in talking to them, just telling me what he thinks is wrong.

As I'm writing this, I've realized that when I put boundaries in place on what I'm willing to listen to from him, it severely limits our conversations. In the last two years, I've made a few comments about my childhood and where things should have been different, and he's quick to get off the phone. He's never willing to consider that he did anything wrong by not helping my sister and me with our mother or trying to be better himself.

I have been no contact with my mother since 2023. I think she moved out in April, and I have had minimal contact with her since. About two months after she moved, I met up with her to give her one of the dogs we had. This dog had really bonded with her, and she wanted to take her, but also wanted to get settled first. She tried to get us to stop by her apartment, but I instead met her at the PetSmart parking lot.

We chatted for about 5 minutes, and I made up an excuse to leave. That was the last time I saw her in person. In August of 2023, she texted me on my birthday with a message about how she loved me, whether I liked it or not. I replied that words like these are why I'm distancing myself from her.

After that, I heard nothing again until this past August when she again wished me a happy birthday, and I thanked her. Is there more I'd like to say? Of course, there is. There are days I'd like to reach out and talk to her like I used to. But I won't. For my own personal happiness, I won't. Reaching out to her in any way will invite all of it back in. She's not gone to therapy or done any work to figure out what went wrong.

I know from hearing it from others that she has stated that she has no idea what happened. And that's fine. That's her story to tell and not one I'm willing to work to discredit. I know my truth, and that's all that matters. My sister is in contact with her, and I know I'll be told when she passes, but I'm entirely content for that to happen without my seeing her one last time. She will not apologize for any pain that she's caused me, and I'm not going to try to get that. My personal mental health is more important to me.

I still deal with lingering thoughts of how I should be making sure she's ok, or making sure she has what she needs to be happy because that's what I was conditioned to do, but I push them away with my mantra…she's a grown assed adult. I should never have been responsible for her happiness, and I should never have put her needs above my own and those of my family.

It's not right for me to have to talk myself down from taking care of her over myself, and I know that I'm being good for me when I don't. I'm sad for the situation she's put herself in, living alone in a new state with very few friends and family for support, but again…she's a grown assed adult. She is capable of doing better for herself, and she's able to seek help to build a healthier human. She won't, but she could. She's sought therapy a few times, but for therapy to work, you have to be willing to be ugly and honest about who you are and what choices you're making. It is my opinion that she'll never be ready to do that. She'll turn 77 next year, and I just don't think she has it in her to turn over that leaf now. If losing my family didn't get her there, I don't know that anything will.

As for my family, I told my kids that they are free to have a relationship with their grandmother if that's what they choose. I told them I was making my decision for my personal health and that they should too. Sadly, they witnessed the end of the end firsthand, and they also experienced weird things with their own relationships with her that none of them talk to her today.

She sends them Venmo cash on their birthdays, and they thank her, but that's it. She's tried to post things on my daughter's social pages, and in turn, my youngest has reached out to tell her that's inappropriate, considering they don't talk in real life. She never heard anything from my mother after that comment.

As a grandmother, I have no understanding of how you could walk away from your grandchildren, but she's walked away from her daughter as well, and I can't imagine that either. It's heartbreaking, but I know we've raised strong children, and they fully understand that just because you're related by blood, it doesn't mean you're meant to be in one another's lives.

Almost none of our mutual family and friends have reached out to me to see why my mother and I don't talk. I'm not sure if that's because she's told horrible stories about me, or maybe they just aren't curious or don't even know. I have one second cousin who tried to shame me in a Facebook comment, and I mentioned that she may not know the whole story, and maybe she should research before she speaks. I never heard anything further. I'm probably going to send her a copy of this book once it's published, so maybe she will learn a thing or two about the woman she considers a wonderful aunt. Not that my mother probably wasn't wonderful to that cousin, but she sure wasn't her true self around her! That was reserved for those of us who lived with her!

I am at peace with my decisions regarding my relationships with my parents. I wish like hell that they could be different for me, but I'm not willing to set myself aside any longer to attempt to have a connection. I'm more important than that. And I deserve more. I was talking to a friend recently who has very similar parents, and she stated, "They did the best they could". I took that moment to tell her there was a little bit better way to phrase that. In my opinion, my parents did what they thought was right at the time. They didn't do their best, or they would have taken the time to do the work to make themselves better for their children.

They didn't try to be close to me in the correct ways then, and they don't try to understand who I am today, or have relationships with my family, and that's their loss. It's heartbreaking, honestly, but it's not for me to fix. These people are grown assed adults, and they did what they did.

I choose to be healthier for my family, I choose to admit when I'm wrong, and I try hard to make it up to my children when I upset them. I'm willing to listen and try where my parents aren't and weren't. I am the parent I wished I had been given growing up, and that must be enough. I broke the cycle for my kids, and I've given them a different experience. In no way has my parenting been perfect, but I know they're less damaged than I am!

And family looks a little bit different, too. My husband's best friend and his family have become the people we look to for unconditional love. His parents have given me some of the best hugs of my life, and I've talked to them so much over the last few years. They parented their children so much differently than my parents did, and they both have supported us in the boundaries I've put in place with my parents. His sister looks after us like we're her own, and I feel so much love in their presence. We've joined them for numerous holiday celebrations that are free from the eggshell angst of my past life.

It's blissful just to experience love without all the other bullshit. These people have been in our lives since I met my husband in 1999, but since walking away from my mother, they've come to mean so much more. Society tells us that we have to treat our parents with love and respect, but it fails to put the same onus on parents.

It's like the children we're told to be responsible for upkeeping that relationship, but I'm here to tell you that's not really necessary. It's terrific if you have parents who cultivate a relationship with you just as much as you do with them, but it's ok if that's not your reality.

Putting boundaries in place with blood relatives that protect your peace needs to be widely accepted as perfectly fine. Personal mental health is more important than blood, and family should be anyone you want to include in your life.

Chapter Six:
My Sister and I

After going no contact with my mother, my sister and I really started talking about our childhood. For close to 48 years, I had no conscious understanding that my mother and father were narcissists. I did not understand all the things my sister had gone through in her childhood that had been nothing like mine, even though we lived in the same house with the same parents.

I had no idea why we were never close and why when we fought, it seemed like my parents pleaded for us to start speaking again, while at the same time telling tales on the other that further drove a wedge in our relationship. It's been miserable. My sister has been married twice, and I was only invited to her second ceremony. I have missed decades of having a relationship with my sister because of my parents. After college, my sister went through difficult times with her mental health, and I was barely aware or able to help because we were never encouraged to be close.

There's nothing I can reference to say we ever drifted apart. I don't think there was ever enough together between my sister and me to drift apart. We were beside each other for dinners and vacations, but we were rarely together.

I have no memories of playing together or being encouraged to be sisterly, like I've seen in my friends with sisters. I just don't think it happened. I don't think my parents ever thought to encourage us to be together.

I don't know why we didn't latch on to one another in a protective kind of way, but that just wasn't the case. In my strange, gappy memory of my life, I just don't have any recollection of a defining moment where we decided not to be close; we just never were.

Listening to my sister's stories over the past two years has shown me that there was so much happening right in my own home that I was completely unaware of. I know there's a part of me that ignored my sister and my parents because I didn't want to be part of the theater aspect of their lives. Still, I had no idea my parents so significantly overstepped boundaries with my sister in ways that forever impacted her mental health and well-being.

I'm trying not to go into too much detail because these are my sister's stories to tell, but my parents both confided in her their intimate thoughts and feelings about one another, the death of my grandparents, and their life in general. My sister shouldn't have been told so many things over the years, and more importantly, she should have been shown how to put boundaries in place with people who should have known better. She was a child, and her parents should have protected her.

At this point, I would say that my sister and I are closer now than we ever have been. We talk a few times a month and share life details. I do feel like we're both still pretty guarded with one another, and I wish that weren't the case.

I think we've also "trauma bonded" now that I know the whole truth, and that's so sad. We were never the priority, and the love we were given was completely conditional. I know my self-esteem is still a significant struggle for me, and I know she's had to work on that diligently as well.

My sister has contact with both our parents, but seems to limit it for her own well-being. She sees them a couple of times a year and tries to talk to them weekly.

But I feel like we're honestly just waiting for them to pass away so that their stress will die with them. I hope that when they're gone, the need to compete for their love will stop. I hope that my sister and I can find our own happiness with one another so that we can build a new type of bond that doesn't come with narcissistic strings attached.

I would be lying if I didn't say I'm worried when they're gone, we won't have anything to talk about, but I'm hoping we'll find new avenues for our friendship. It would be devastating for the damage my parents inflicted to sustain after they are no longer. I'm going to work very hard to ensure that doesn't happen.

Chapter Seven:
Where Are My Parents

My parents live in different states, over six hours away from me. They both turned 76 this year, and I know neither is overly healthy. They've struggled with weight and other issues of growing old. I see so many of my friends taking care of their aging parents, and I'm not involved. My sister talks to both weekly and fills me in on how they are, but it reminds me of hearing about a far-off family member or friend. I just don't have the connection to them that I used to, and that's because I stopped allowing the manipulation. We never had a loving relationship; these people weren't for me what I am to my kids.

They needed me to behave a certain way to have attention, and when I stopped playing my part, I stopped hearing from them. It's crazy to me that I exist in the world and seldom interact with my parents. There are plenty of times when guilt comes over me, but then I ask myself why they aren't feeling the same guilt for not seeing or talking to me? And the answer to that is what keeps me at peace.

They aren't worried about me, so there's no need for me to worry about them. It's never been a give-and-take, so why should it be just because they're old? As I type this, I know it will sound cold to someone who doesn't have a narcissistic parent, but it's just the truth. Why should I let go of my peace because they won't be around much longer? I have worked hard to build myself and my life to the place it is today, and I've done so without their drama. I'm not willing to take a step back into that now.

My mom lives in North Carolina with her dog. For so much of my life, she seemed to be an amazing mom. We saw each other at events…dinners out, school events for my kids, and at church. Places where other people were watching. She prided herself on showing up and showing how much she loved us. She smiled and volunteered at my kid's school, and she did so much to support my family. I called her daily…sometimes more than once. I called for good things and for bad. I called when I was driving just to catch up. I enjoyed doing things with her, and I hardly remembered the years before I turned 20 and had no idea that she was the root of so much of my inner angst. I miss her daily.

I miss having that mom, but as I described earlier in the book…living with her changed everything. It was like pulling back the curtain on the wizard. The woman she is isn't the mom I need. She's not healthy for me, and she's not someone I'm willing to have in my life.

After walking away from my mom, my youngest daughter told me that the last year of living together, my mom had hardly had anything to do with her. This was my daughter's senior year of high school, and she lived in the same house as someone who barely spoke to her. In elementary school, my mom used to meet her bus, and they'd spend afternoons together shopping or running errands.

Things out in public where others could see her as the doting grandmother. Living in the same house, they became strangers. It made me so sad to know that my daughter had gone through this with someone who used to show her attention and affection. I know I am damaged by the relationships I had with my parents, but to know my daughter is too hurts me so much worse.

At this point, I am in contact with my dad, but we don't talk often. He lives in South Carolina, and I usually see him about once a year. My dad has never pretended to be anything other than what he is, so while the hurt is less, the damage is still real. He wasn't present in my life very often then, and he's not really present in my life now.

We text about the weather, he tells me about his dogs and his lawn and things he's spent money on, but real heartfelt conversations don't happen often. I've tried to tell him things and ask him to be supportive or congratulatory for different things, and the response I get is lackluster and often isn't worth the effort. Oh, and we talk college or NFL football. He follows Alabama and the University of South Carolina, while I favor the Oregon Ducks. If you haven't guessed, these are all safe topics that don't go very deep. That's pretty par for the course, but still sad.

One thing my father loves more than anything is money. He worked very hard and made sound financial decisions, and he's very well off. If you ask him, though, he's basically down to his last nickel. Growing up, my father was always in a payment plan with his parents. I realized that he used them as a personal bank. He'd go buy a car, get financing from the dealer, and a month later, he'd pay it off with money he'd borrow from his parents.

The loan terms were always much more favorable, very low interest, and as far as the credit bureaus knew, he had very little debt. I honestly thought that was the way family finances worked for a very long time. But once I became an adult, I learned that his rules were very different. He hates to loan out his money. He will freely spend money on himself but complains constantly about spending on household or life necessities. And forget needing money as his daughter.

There were times when my kids were little that a small loan here or there was needed. I liken it to borrowing money from the devil. He wouldn't just lend it with a repayment plan; he'd offer to skip your birthday or Christmas presents for however long it took to "repay" that amount.

Now I'm sure it should sound like that's great…getting money without having to repay it. But losing a gift hurt more than paying back a loan. It's always a bargain, and usually, if I went to him to ask, it's because we needed the funds and not because I was buying myself something nice or spending frivolously.

For as long as I can remember, he's talked about how much money will be left to my sister and me when he's gone. A close family friend has a completely different view on money and his kids. He's also very well off and gives his kids cash constantly. He shares in small windfalls from the sale of this or that, or he just provides as needed. His take on this is that he'd rather see his kids happy while he's alive to enjoy life with them. Makes me shake my head. The narcissistic way of preening about how much he has while sitting high on his pile of money is much more my father's way.

Friends of mine have lost their parents, and my most significant fear is that I won't be that sad when my parents pass. I'm afraid I will experience emotions like relief or apathy. Numbness or worse, just nothing. I know I will attend and most likely coordinate my parents' funerals with my sister.

I worry that I will be frustrated with everyone around me talking about what amazing people my parents were. I've been asked if I had any final thoughts that I'd love to share with my parents before they go, but really, I don't. You can't explain to a narcissist what they did that hurt you. My parents are so far gone on believing they're own lies that anything I say wouldn't be heard.

I know that I have been a wonderful daughter for as long as I was playing my part, and I know that I'm still a wonderful daughter even though I don't anymore. I deserved to be loved in a way that is healthy for me, and I don't have to have people in my life who can't abide by that. After going no contact with my mom, I got a tattoo on my arm to remind me of where I find peace. It's the word Strength with two small fences on either side. The fences represent boundaries. And by erecting tiny fences in my mind or using my words with people, I am putting up safe boundaries that protect my mental health from others. It's never easy to do, but once you start and you let yourself feel the healing power that comes from choosing yourself first, it makes such a difference.

Episode III:
The Finale

I have always wanted to write a book. I never knew what I was going to write about, even though I really felt I had a story in here somewhere. The idea for this book was to help someone feel like they're not alone if they came from a life where both of their parents are narcissists. It's an interesting dynamic and one I'm still working at being ok with. Usually, there's a bad parent and a good one. The good one might be weak because they let the narcissist behave poorly, but that good one gives love and affection to the best of their ability.

When you grow up without that piece, you seek it in other places: teachers, friends, chosen family. You eventually might learn to find it in yourself if you do the work to get there. Obviously, that's the ultimate goal. Because, as a child of a narcissist, you're taught that your thoughts and feelings are always second to theirs. You are conditioned to believe that what they want in life is the top priority, and I was taught that keeping them happy was my job.

As an adult, I believed I had to keep everyone happy. My kids, my husband, the teachers, the coaches, all of the people in my orbit. I volunteered for all the things. I was the room mom and the team mom. I made the signs, did the projects with my kids, took things to school, and tried to sign up to help as often as I could so that people would like me. For the longest time, I didn't believe I was likable all by myself. I thought I had to do good things in order to earn the love and affection of others. That's bullshit. I am lovable without doing anything. And so are you. I am important, and I should not put my wants and needs aside for anyone.

At times, that requires a lot of juggling to get what I need and what others need to align, but learning to do that with grace and forgiveness is an amazing feeling. I had to teach myself to stop thinking it was my JOB to make everyone else happy and to put everyone else's wants and needs above my own. It's such a myth in today's world that women have to be all and do all in order to be liked or loved. It's not necessary.

Do the things that give your heart joy and say no when they don't. It took me forever to realize that by putting myself last, I was never truly happy. For so long, I believed that my happiness was derived from how others saw me, and it's just not. I like fifty-three-year-old me. And I'm a very likable person. Am I everyone's cup of tea? No, but we really shouldn't be. In my opinion, if you're everyone's cup of tea, you're actually giving away too much of yourself to be healthy.

I'm way more at peace and mentally stable today than I ever have been, but I'm still triggered at times and have to take time to chat with myself about what's going on. I have a phenomenal therapist that I can reach out to when things get a little past my ability to talk to myself, and I frequently tell my husband probably way more than he wants to hear about something that freaked me out! For instance, we recently were headed out on a Saturday evening to attend a birthday party. I work from home and don't see people as often as I once did.

I'd been looking forward to the party and celebrating the birthday girl, but as we drove there, I started to panic about the whole thing and wanted to turn around! I worried that I'd have to be "on stage" in the social situation and that I'd have to pretend. I started totally freaking out internally while still signing along to the radio and appearing fine on the outside. Then I stopped. I told my husband how I was feeling, and we talked about the fact that the party was for someone I adored and that my favorite cousins would be there too. These cousins are some of the strongest people I have in my blood family, and they've never apologized for who they are.

They've also never asked me to be anything other than who I am, and they've stood by me through many ugly parts of my life. By the time we arrived, I felt stronger, and we ended up having a great night. But it took time to talk myself through all the emotions that came out of nowhere, and that's ok. Sometimes we need to have a little chat to get through things, and there's nothing wrong with that. Sometimes triggers come up when you least expect them, and it's how you handle them that matters. Not that you have them or that they bring a pause, but what you choose to do about them. I don't have to pretend to be anything anymore. I can just be me, and if part of that is telling my husband I'm freaking out and want to go home, it's fine. Had it been really bad, he'd have taken me home, but this time I was able to talk it out and be ok.   I am strong, and he loves me, and any decision I needed would have been the one we went with.   I cannot tell you how emotionally freeing that is.

I love to read and research.   I want to understand what I'm feeling and how that fits in with all the other people and their feelings.   I want to make things make sense, and I hope this book has done that.   I hope it's made you think about where you are in life and what you want to do differently.   I did not write this book to tell you I've figured it all out and provide you the yellow brick road of life, or even pull back the curtain and introduce you to Oz.   I just wanted to tell my story and let you see how it makes you feel.

If reading this book has made you feel less alone than it was worth my time to write it. Suppose you see yourself or your situation in my words, welcome.   You are not alone.   You are not crazy, and you are enough. You don't have to stay stuck in the middle of your narcissistic parents; you can step out of their shadows and become the person you are meant to be!   If you think I'm full of shit and that I've spent all these pages whining about an otherwise acceptable life, then I encourage you to think about finding a therapist.   You've got a lot of work to do if you read this far and hate me.

Episode IV:
Random Thoughts

So many unexpected life philosophies have come from my experiences with therapy and going no contact with my parents. A few of my favorites are below, and I hope some of them resonate with you. I genuinely believe I am who I am because of my journey. I don't think I'd tell my younger self to do anything different except love herself more. I believe that I've gone on this road to get to where I am and the loves I have in my life, and I wouldn't trade any part of that. Maybe just read through these final thoughts and see if any of them speak to you on your journey.

Healing never happens overnight. It happens only as fast as you work at it and only if you're able to be honest with yourself about how deep the damage goes.

Triggering moments are EVERYWHERE. Even when you think you've got it all figured out, you'll still be vibing through life and run across something that dredges up some awful moment from the past. Learning to sit with it for a moment and move through the feeling instead of ignoring it is so much healthier. Please just trust me on this. I've tried the other way, and it's so time-consuming, and you just have to continue to do it over until you do it right!

Going limited or no contact with a parent is not something done overnight, out of spite, or to teach a lesson. It's not easy, and it hurts like hell. It's a survival tactic, and you have to be willing to live with missing that person or the person you wish they were. By going no contact with my mother, I'm protecting myself and my mental health, but every single day I want to call her and tell her something like I used to do before I knew who she really was.

Therapists are people too. Some of them are really good for you, and some aren't. You honestly have to weed through until you find that one that gives you the space and guidance to do the work on who you are to be able to stand firm for that inner person. It's ok to keep playing the field until you find Mr. or Mrs. Right. They'll understand, and if they don't, they're for sure NOT the one you need!

Meds are ok. Taking prescribed medication to assist your mental health is not being weak, it's not giving in, and it's not something to be ashamed of. It's a tool in your box to help you be the best version of yourself. It's not "drug seeking" to ask for something to assist what's happening in your head. Sometimes people need a little something to take the edge off of life, and it's much healthier, in my opinion, to be prescribed something than it is to try the self-medication route. Not that wine or a gummy isn't also a viable option in that toolbox <wink, wink>, but I don't believe they're the best way to mitigate your thoughts daily.

Everything I've written in this book is my thoughts and feelings on the life I've lived and how I've chosen to handle these situations. When I meet a new parent, I tell them to parent in the way that works best for them and their children. Don't do things because you read it or someone else tells you it must be that way. I feel the same way about mental health and boundaries. Do what works for you and your loved ones. Do what keeps you healthy and happy. Don't stay stuck because society or parental guilt says that's the way it should be. Be strong enough to get yourself unstuck and know that in all things you are the most important one and you are always enough!

www.ingramcontent.com/pod-product-compliance
Lightning Source LLC
Chambersburg PA
CBHW041650150726
48005CB00013BA/1608